Help your students
find and follow
God's calling in their
vocations

[So what am I gonna do with my LIFE?]

Help your students
find and follow
God's calling in their
vocations

[So what am I gonna do with my LIFE?]

Diane Lindsey Reeves

Youth Specialties

ZondervanPublishingHouse
Grand Rapids, Michigan

A Division of HarperCollinsPublishers

CONTENTS

How to USE this book

So what am I gonna do with my life?

It's an age-old question everyone gets to answer sooner or later. For Christian young people the question has an added dimension—what does *God* want me to do with my life?
It's a big question.

It's also one that causes many young people to flounder as they try to figure out life after high school. Somehow our culture and—to a large degree—our churches have made this inevitable life transition seem like a mysterious rite of passage. Of course, the teen years are so wrought with potential disaster that when our students get through safely, we breathe a collective sigh of relief, shoo them out the door into adulthood, and wish them well. When it comes to youth ministry, surviving the present is tantamount to facing the future. Yet, apart from guiding young people toward a commitment to Christ, helping them find their destiny is one of the most important contributions we can make in their lives.

That's why the **Leader's Guide** for this four-week series of sessions—along with three **After Hours** sessions and the *So What Am I Gonna Do with My Life? Journaling Workbook for Students*—is jam-packed with ideas, activities, and thought-provoking discussions to point youths toward productive and satisfying futures. In particular this curriculum—

- Incorporates practical experiences while imparting eternal truths.
- Balances fun peer interaction with opportunities for serious personal soul-searching.
- Builds upon the kinship and concern that's part of growing up in the family of God.

So What Am I Gonna Do with My Life? is not Sunday school lite. It introduces a hard-hitting, life-changing process. Fainthearted students need not apply.

And that goes for youth leaders and program directors as well. To get the full impact of the program you'll have to do a little extra legwork yourself—reaching out to the community, involving the church family, engaging in earnest discussions with mixed-up teens. (What's new about that?)

Using *So What Am I Gonna Do with My Life?* will give you a break from the routine topics and lessons your teens might be used to, but success requires a thoughtful commitment from all who embark on this quest. Think of it as short-term pain for long-term gain—an investment in the futures of your youths.

So instead of watching your teens wallow in uncertainty, waiting for the proverbial bolt of lightning to strike them with *the call*, you can help them—

- Explore what God's Word says about fulfilling his will in all of life's important decisions.
- Seek answers to their questions about their futures.
- Make the most of their God-given abilities and opportunities.
- Allow others to invest in their lives.
- Make commitments to fully invest in their futures.

In the **Leader's Guide,** the sessions include several common elements to make it easy to organize and prepare for your time with students.

- **The Big Plan** is a concise summary of the main theme of the session.
- **The Whole Truth** lists if-you-don't-get-anything-else-out-of-the-session-get-this ideas.
- **What the Good Book Says** contains Bible verses that support the theme and key message of each session.
- **Your Biblical Mentors** comprises Bible characters who have faced similar issues with varying degrees of success, whom you can expose your students to.

You are taken through the sessions step by step, using discussions, activities, and games to introduce, teach, reinforce, and apply the main ideas. Of course, you know your students and their needs better than anyone else, so adapt the sessions to meet your requirements.

- **The 411** provides leaders with background information and statistics to introduce each topic.
- **Getting the Mood Right** suggests music selections to use before, during, or after each session to reinforce key messages.
- **Goofing Off** offers a warm-up activity to get students mingling and ready to focus on the lesson at hand.
- **Kicking Things Off** offers a skit, ice-breaker, or other attention-getting activity to get rolling and introduce the main point of the session.
- **Going Deeper** provides ideas for group discussion and small group activities that help students discover Scriptural truths and principles.
- **Keepin' It Real** takes the process further with small group activities that give students the chance to apply truths in their own lives.
- **No Time Like the Present** offers practical, nitty-gritty kinds of activities to help students connect truths with real-life situations and opportunities.
- **Buckling Down** encourages small group discussions of students' weekly progress in their journals.
- **Futurama** is your opportunity to advertise upcoming sessions and **After Hours** activities. Check out **The Buzz Factor** promotional postcards and fliers (pages 65-75)!
- **The Finish Line** is a brief time for your students to pray together in small groups.

After Hours are supplemental activities designed to nudge young people out into the world to explore occupational opportunities—go-for-the-gusto and let-your-light-shine inspiration. Who doesn't need some of that?

The activities are meant to teach real-life skills in a fun way. The challenge is creating a safe place to explore. No idea is too crazy to plumb; no dream too audacious to pursue.

- **Save Room for the Smorgasbord!** is a snoop-your-way-to-success event that includes idea-generating activities, a library scavenger hunt, and Net surfing. All with the aim of making informed choices.
- **Grabbing Tried and True Tips from Familiar Faces** allows the whole church to get involved in a career fair—sharing information about their professions, encouraging youths, and offering support. It's a great way to bridge the generation gap—for an evening, at least!
- **Only the Shadow Knows...** enables your students to get firsthand experiences in various work environments, where they can find out what they like and don't like. Send your group out into the workplace for a day, then bring them back together for a show-and-tell debriefing.

Do all three **After Hours** events or mix and match the activities as time and interest allow. Use them as part of your regular youth group meetings or offer them as extra support for seniors or students who are game for preparing for life after high school.

Even though you can help your students with many aspects of their career hunts, they must think through issues and feelings on their own, too. Ultimately, the decisions are theirs. That's why *So What Am I Gonna Do with My Life? Journaling Workbook for Students* is part of this curriculum. Each session and the **After Hours** events refer you to corresponding sections of the student journal where teens will find helpful questions, information, Bible studies, and guidance. Encourage your students to use the journals between group sessions or, if you prefer, set aside personal time during group sessions for journal writing.

Enjoy the challenge of inspiring your students with *So What Am I Gonna Do with My Life?*

After you've FRAMED your DIPLOMA

[The 411]

Work was designed by none other than God himself as an important part of human experience. After a busy week creating all things great and small, one of God's final acts of creation was to put a man in the Garden of Eden to work and take care of it (Genesis 2:15).

The original idea seemed to be that work was good. Probably much like our idea of play. Satisfying. Fun. A reason to get up in the morning. And it was a means to honor God. Adam's first job was to name all the animals God had created: hagfish, komodo dragons, bandicoots, duck-billed platypuses, gibbons, and the like. We're talking goofy stuff!

Then came the fall of man. That's when work became more like the four-letter word it's sometimes known as today. However there's no indication God's original intention for work ever changed. Work was—and is—a good thing. Not necessarily easy, but good. An essential part of life on earth. The Bible frequently mentions people engaged in meaningful, sustaining work pursuits: shepherds, government leaders, priests, soldiers, farmers, tentmakers—to name a few. In fact Scripture often *defines* people by the type of work they did: David the king, Luke the physician, Joseph the carpenter.

As you start this process of guiding your students toward finding God's purposes in their own work choices, never forget God is famous for things like making the last into the first and the least into the most. Be open to the unique possibilities God has in store for your kids.

The Big Plan

Find God's best plan for your life's work and discover real success.

The Whole Truth

- *God ordains work as part of the human experience.*
- *While God sometimes uses dramatic means to reveal his plans, he tends to use more subtle methods: the truth revealed in his Word, the godly counsel of wise believers, and the open door of opportunity.*
- *God's definition of success may be different from human definitions.*

What the Good Book Says

- *Exodus 3:2-12*
- *1 Samuel 3:1-14*
- *Acts 9:1-20*
- *James 4:13-15*

Your Biblical Mentors

- *Moses*
- *Samuel*
- *Paul*

[Getting the Mood Right]

You might want to play some music that will help your students process the key messages. Consider playing some of the following songs before, during, or after the session:

- "Place in This World" recorded by Michael W. Smith on the album *Go West Young Man* (Reunion, 1991)
- "Help Me God" recorded by Kathy Troccoli on the album *Love and Mercy* (Reunion, 1997)
- "Consider the Choices" recorded by Clay Crosse on the album *Stained Glass* (Reunion, 1997)

GOOFING OFF

The Oldest PROFESSIONS

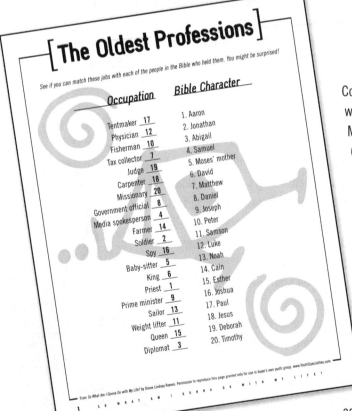

[The Oldest Professions]

See if you can match these jobs with each of the people in the Bible who held them. You might be surprised!

Occupation

Occupation	
Tentmaker	17
Physician	12
Fisherman	10
Tax collector	7
Judge	19
Carpenter	18
Missionary	20
Government official	8
Media spokesperson	4
Farmer	14
Soldier	2
Spy	16
Baby-sitter	5
King	6
Priest	1
Prime minister	9
Sailor	13
Weight lifter	11
Queen	15
Diplomat	3

Bible Character

1. Aaron
2. Jonathan
3. Abigail
4. Samuel
5. Moses' mother
6. David
7. Matthew
8. Daniel
9. Joseph
10. Peter
11. Samson
12. Luke
13. Noah
14. Cain
15. Esther
16. Joshua
17. Paul
18. Jesus
19. Deborah
20. Timothy

[You'll need]

- Pencils
- Bibles
- Bible concordances, handbooks, or dictionaries
- Copies of **The Oldest Professions** (page 16), one for each student

Connect the idea of work with the Christian walk through a simple warm-up activity. Make copies of **The Oldest Professions** (page 16). This worksheet includes two lists: the names of Bible characters and a variety of occupations. The object of this activity is to match the character with the correct occupation.

Give students a copy as they arrive and let them see how many they can figure out. Hints from in-the-know youth leaders, a good Bible concordance, Bible handbook, Bible dictionary, or advice from kids who actually paid attention during their childhood Sunday school lessons are all acceptable ways to gather information. The correct matches for the **The Oldest Professions** are at left.

THEATER
Talk

You'll need

- Four volunteer actors prepared for the skit
- Three cozy chairs, a scrapbook, night clothes (optional), and any other props necessary to give the set a homey look
- Copies of **The Talk** (page 17) script for the cast only

If possible, officially start the session by darkening the room, theater-style. Then have your well-rehearsed volunteer thespians act out **The Talk** (page 17) to introduce the major life transition looming ahead for your students.

GOD'S WILL—
find it here!

After the skit start a discussion about how getting a life after high school might be quite a bit different from life as they've known it so far. Mention how the lives of average teens are just that—*average*. They eat and sleep in a house someone else pays for. They go to a school someone else tells them to go to and work on projects someone else assigns. Toss in some sports activities, a part-time job or two, and some fun with friends and you pretty much have it—the life of the average teen. Their roles are, for the most part, pretty well defined—student, friend, sibling, and son or daughter.

Once kids cross that infamous portal into adulthood (does anyone really know where that is?), things get more complicated. The choices grow in incredible—and sometimes incredibly scary—ways. College—which college and what major? Military—which branch and what specialty? Job—where and how? Marry—who and when? In short, *what do you want to be when you grow up?*

For Christians the best answers are found in finding and following God's direction in life. When things get harried, it's great comfort to know *someone* has a plan. Someone who has our best interests at heart. Someone who's already seen the end of the play and knows how it turns out.

If possible, relate your own story of how God has "worked things together for good" in your own life. Be frank about struggles and mistakes. Describe how the pieces have fallen together in ways you couldn't have planned.

Let them know God has a future planned for them that only they can accomplish. Something that will make the most of their talents, interests, and abilities. Something that—corny as it may sound—

will help them fulfill their destiny on earth. (Cool!)

The only catch is they have to figure out what it is.

Good thing that God has ways of letting us in on his plans. For instance, take a look at how God revealed his plans to men like Jacob, Moses, Gideon, Samuel, Jonah, and Paul. Assign small groups or individuals a character and corresponding Scripture passage listed on **God's Will—Find It Here!** (page 18). Have them read the passages to discover how God revealed his will in those situations. When you bring your students back together, allow them to share their findings.

- **Jacob**—Genesis 28:10-22, 32:22-30
- **Moses**—Exodus 3:2-12
- **Gideon**—Judges 6:36-40
- **Samuel**—1 Samuel 3:1-14
- **Jonah**—Jonah 1:1-17
- **Paul**—Acts 9:1-20

Now contrast God's extraordinary communication with Bible characters and these principles about finding God's will:

Zap!

If you have the time, skills, and equipment, you may want to put together a video or skit using youth leaders or students in the youth group. The topic should focus on hopes for the future and may include the subjects getting zapped with God's guidance by things like a lightning bolt, a brick, or a booming voice from above.

*Adapted from **Decision Making and the Will of God** by Garry Friesen and J. Robin Maxson (Multnomah Press, 1980).*

1. The Bible reveals commands and principles about God's will that we are to obey (God's moral will).
2. Christians are free to make choices when no relevant command or principle is in Scripture (nonmoral decisions).
3. In nonmoral decisions, Christians should aim to make wise choices, using a combination of signs including the Bible, common sense, personal desires, wise counsel, answered prayer, circumstances, and inner impressions.
4. In all decisions, Christians should humbly submit to God's will.

Since choosing a career is most often a nonmoral decision, focusing on the third principle is helpful. Hand students or small groups strips with Bible verses from the bottom of **God's Will—Find It Here!** Have students determine the road sign that is useful for determining God's will in mostly nonmoral situations like deciding careers. Guide students in discussing how and why these road signs are useful.

- **The Bible**—Psalm 119:105; 2 Timothy 3:16-17
- **Common sense**—Proverbs 3:21
- **Personal desire**—Psalm 37:4
- **Wise counsel**—Proverbs 13:20
- **Answered prayers**—John 16:23-24
- **Circumstances**—Philippians 4:11
- **Inner impressions (peace)**—John 14:27

Tell them that you'll be exploring more about how to find and follow God's will in the workplace throughout these sessions.

KEEPIN' IT REAL
Gotcha COVERED

Throughout this book whiteboard and markers are listed for activities that require writing for the entire group's viewing. Of course you can also use an overhead projector and markers, a flipchart, butcher paper taped on the wall, or whatever other resources are available.

You'll need
- Whiteboard
- Markers

When it comes to following God's will, there are a few things you don't have to worry about. God has already given clear instructions about what he wants you to do—or not do. Help your group generate a list of activities that are clearly God's will for his children, then write this list on a whiteboard or other place everyone can see. Here's a handful to get you started—

- **Living a holy life**—1 Thessalonians 4:7
- **Practicing self-control**—1 Peter 5:8

- **Asking for and giving forgiveness**—Matthew 6:14; 1 John 1:9
- **Worshiping God**—Psalm 100:2
- **Confessing your sins**—1 John 1:9
- **Having a Christlike attitude**—Philippians 2:5
- **Serving one another**—Galatians 5:13

You're It!

*If you feel like your group is fairly evenly matched in spiritual maturity, you may want to add some fun to **Gotcha Covered** with a "tag, you're it" element. Pick someone to give the first response, and then have that person physically tag the next student to answer. [You might consider switching from person to person by throwing a Nerf ball or some other creative item to keep the game moving in a fast-paced, attention-grabbing way.]*

NO TIME LIKE THE PRESENT
Spell CHECK

You'll need
- Two large sheets of paper or poster board
- Markers
- Bibles

Scary as their futures may seem, your students can trust God to have their best interests at heart— always. Genuine success is his desire for all. The catch is in how he defines success. It may be a little different from the way most people define it.

Divide the group in half and give each a huge sheet of paper with the word SUCCESS written on it. Ask one group to define success as *people*—the world in general—might see it while the other group defines it as *God* would see it. Students may prefer writing the definition in the form of an acronym. Have Bibles available and encourage them to back up God's definition of success with Scripture.

After the groups give an informal presentation of their definitions, you might want to wrap up the activity by sharing one or more of the following verses: Joshua 1:8; Proverbs 3:1-6; and Matthew 5:1-12.

Give students copies of *So What Am I Gonna Do with My Life? Journaling Workbook for Students* and encourage them to invest some time in their future by completing the following brief assignments before the next session (pages 9-17 in the journal):

- **To Be or Not to Be** *Let your students discover who they are and what that has to do with their future.*
- **First Impressions** *This think-fast exercise will help students unlock secret stuff they may never have known about themselves.*
- **Pile It On!** *How to make a good life—hold the pickles, please.*
- **Everybody Has a Story** *Your students will get to look into the stories of those around them and find out if they have happy endings.*
- **The Word on Work** *What the world's wisest man had to say about work—it's not just a four-letter word, you know.*
- **Christians at Work** *Angela Elwell Hunt—an author who put her gift of gab to work in over 76 books!*

Let your students know the group will be discussing the journal assignments during the next meeting. Since journaling is personal, let them know they only have to share what they're comfortable talking about.

FUTURAMA

Promote the next session of *So What Am I Gonna Do with My Life?* and the upcoming **After Hours** event you're planning— perhaps through a brief skit, video commercial, or flier. See page 19 for details on the next session and pages 49-64 for **After Hours** ideas. Reproducible postcards for promotion are on pages 65-75.

THE FINISH LINE

Conclude this session by having students gather in groups of twos or threes to pray for each other as they continue their quests to find God's direction in their lives.

[The Oldest Professions]

See if you can match these jobs with each of the people in the Bible who held them. You might be surprised!

_____ Occupation	Bible Character _____
Tentmaker _____	1. Aaron
Physician _____	2. Jonathan
Fisherman _____	3. Abigail
Tax collector _____	4. Samuel
Judge _____	5. Moses' mother
Carpenter _____	6. David
Missionary _____	7. Matthew
Government official _____	8. Daniel
Media spokesperson _____	9. Joseph
Farmer _____	10. Peter
Soldier _____	11. Samson
Spy _____	12. Luke
Baby-sitter _____	13. Noah
King _____	14. Cain
Priest _____	15. Esther
Prime minister _____	16. Joshua
Sailor _____	17. Paul
Weight lifter _____	18. Jesus
Queen _____	19. Deborah
Diplomat _____	20. Timothy

[The Talk]

Characters
ANNOUNCER, with a loud, deep voice • **DAD,** Archie Bunker type with a heart
MOM, sweet, my-child-can-do-no-wrong type • **LEXI,** looking bored and increasingly confused

Props
Three cozy chairs • A scrapbook • Other props to give the set a homey look (optional) • Night clothes (optional)

Scene
At home sitting in chairs, Mom and Dad with Lexi (slouched in chair), thumbing through a scrapbook.

ANNOUNCER: *(in booming voice from the back of the room)* It's coming. It's unavoidable. It happens to every-one sooner or later. It's the talk. No, not <u>that</u> talk. <u>This</u> talk… *(turn on lights or shine spotlight on stage)*

DAD: You know, kid, it's been about 18 years now. A really good 18 years. Most of it, anyway. *(shrugging)*

MOM: *(gushing)* Look at what a cute baby you were!

DAD: *(earnestly, without malice)* It sure has been a pleasure working my tail off to put a roof over your head and food in your mouth. I can't think of anything I'd rather have done than worry myself sick about you for the past 18 years.

MOM: *(still gushing)* Oh, here you are on your first day of school!

DAD: All those nights waiting up for you to get home weren't so bad and, gee, even that time I had to pick you up at the police station.

MOM: *(getting protective)* Now, dear…

DAD: It's just that… *(hesitating)*

MOM: You <u>are</u> almost 18 now.

DAD: *(stalling)* So you see, umm…What we're trying to say… *(looking at wife for help)*

MOM: It's nothing personal or anything, sweetie-pie. It's just…it's just… *(looking at husband with uncertainty in her voice)* It's just time for you to…

MOM and DAD: *(standing and shouting with relief)* Get a life!

God's Will—Find It Here!

Jacob—Genesis 28:10-22, 32:22-30

Moses—Exodus 3:2-12

Gideon—Judges 6:36-40

Samuel—1 Samuel 3:1-14

Jonah—Jonah 1:1-17

Paul—Acts 9:1-20

The Bible—Psalm 119:105; 2 Timothy 3:16-17

Common sense—Proverbs 3:21

Personal desire—Psalm 37:4

Wise counsel—Proverbs 13:20

Answered prayers—John 16:23-24

Circumstances—Philippians 4:11

Inner impressions (peace)—John 14:27

He's got YOUR whole DESTINY in his HANDS

[The 411]

Once upon a time career decisions tended to be simple choices—farmer or factory worker? For the more intellectually inclined, options like doctor, lawyer, or banker sweetened the pot. Those days look like a quaint fairly tale to today's generation. Kids now have more choices and more opportunities than ever before.

The Big Plan

You are a unique individual who was created by God with a future planned by God.

The Whole Truth

- *Who you are influences what you should do.*
- *God created you by design and with purpose.*
- *God has big plans for all his children, including you.*
- *God has differend plans for everyone.*

What the Good Book Says

- *Psalm 139:14-16*
- *Proverbs 4:13*
- *Mark 9:35*
- *Romans 8:28*

Your Biblical Mentors

- *Moses*
- *David*
- *Esther*
- *John the Baptist*
- *Peter and Andrew*
- *Paul*

Technology, computers, new modes of transportation, and a fast-paced and ever-changing global economy all conspire to make choosing the right career a mind-boggling experience. Did you know there are more than 20,000 career options to pick from? Did you know many people change careers at least three or four times during their lifetimes to keep pace with all the change? Did you know many of your kids will eventually excel in professions that haven't even been invented yet?

No wonder kids are confused! It's a twist on the Dickens's "best of times, worst of times" sentiment. With that many choices your kids are bound to find some exciting opportunities out there. But with so many choices, where do you start looking?

How about starting at the beginning? Long before these kids were even born. That's when God started making big plans for them. Plans only *they* can live out. He's blessed them with the right stuff to make it happen.

That's why if your kids get to know themselves better, what they do well,

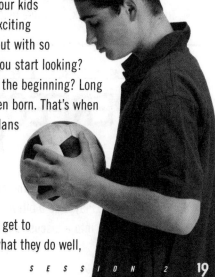

what they like to do, and what they want to do, they'll be well on their way to figuring out what they're meant to do with their lives. No, it's not easy. But with a little help from you, it can be lots of fun!

[Getting the Mood Right]

You might want to play music to help your students process the key messages. Consider playing some of the following songs before, during, or after the session:

- "Moses" recorded by The W's on the album *The W's* (5 Minute Walk, 1998)
- "Trust" recorded by Sixpence None the Richer on the album *The Fatherless and the Widow* (R.E.X., 1993)
- "Let Me Show You the Way" recorded by Michael W. Smith on the album *Live the Life* (Reunion, 1998)
- "My Hope Is You" recorded by Third Day on the album *Conspiracy No. 5* (Reunion, 1997)

GOOFING OFF

TALES too TICKLISH to tell...almost

You'll need
- Some interesting anecdotes about a few kids in your group

Remind kids that they're all one of a kind, even if they have some rather peculiar ways of proving it. Prior to class, make a few phone calls to parents and friends of several kids in the youth group. Find out a funny story or interesting anecdote about each one. Maybe even a goofy hobby or habit. (Be careful about embarrassing anyone inappropriately.) If time is short you can have your kids write down their own stories.

Read a story and let the group guess who it's about. If your students wrote the stories, coach them about not acknowledging their story right away. They can even make a few guesses themselves to throw others off the track. Continue reading stories and guessing.

KICKING THINGS OFF

A PERFECT fit

You'll need
- Two volunteers—one of the largest guys and one of the smallest girls

Ask one of the largest guys and one of the smallest girls to come up to the front. Have them try on each other's shoes. Play it up a bit: *Are they comfortable? What's the problem here? Don't you want to trade?*

Transition into a discussion about how God made us to be one of a kind. Everyone has his or her own talents, traits and interests—the combination of all those things makes each teen one of a kind. Tell them they—just like a rugged tennis shoe or a high-heeled sandal—were all designed for different purposes.

As you move into the discussion, draw out the following points:

- **God likes variety.** Everybody gets a custom plan—just like snowflakes and fingerprints.
- **God likes surprises.** Some of the people you think are the most uncool now will be used to do the most cool things later.
- **God gives you everything you need to do it right.** The talents, the traits, the opportunities—everything is taken care of in God's plan, step by step.

ONE of a kind

You'll need

- Pencils
- Bibles
- A student volunteer to read the Scripture passage
- Copies of **One of a Kind** (page 24), one for each group

Have a student read Psalm 139:14-16 aloud for the group.

> I praise you because I am fearfully and wonderfully made; your works are wonderful, I know that full well. My frame was not hidden from you when I was made in the secret place. When I was woven together in the depths of the earth, your eyes saw my unformed body. All the days ordained for me were written in your book before one of them came to be.
>
> —*Psalm 139:14-16*

Divide the class into groups of three or four. Give each group a copy of **One of a Kind** (page 24), and ask them to use their own words to rewrite the verse in a way that puts their futures in perspective. After they've finished, let a representative from each group read its new version to the rest of the class.

VITAL statistics

You'll need

- Pencils
- Copies of **Vital Statistics** (page 25), one for each student

Provide some tangible proof to your students that they're all one of a kind. Hand out copies of **Vital Statistics** (page 25) to the small groups, and explain that each student needs to personalize the list of

vital stats by finishing the incomplete statements. (Be sure students don't write their names on the worksheets!)

Allow a few minutes for students to work, then have each group gather them up in a pile and mix the papers up. Let students pick worksheets at random (if they get their own, they need to draw again). Have the students guess who wrote each one. Repeat the process until everyone has had a turn.

As you bring the group back together, ask them who in the smaller groups had the same answers to every question on the worksheet. Unless you have Siamese twins in the group, it's highly unlikely—in fact impossible—that any two people would share the same physical characteristics, life experiences, talents, and ambitions. And that's entirely the point.

All those things—what we look like, what we like to do, what we do well, what we really want to do, what our life experience has been—are part of God's plan for our lives.

NO TIME LIKE THE PRESENT

PASS the hat

Though they may have known it before, your teens will have a fresh picture of being one of a kind, unique, designed on purpose, kids with a future—you get the picture. Tell them their uniqueness will come into play

You'll need
- Pencils
- Index cards for every student
- A hat or a box to hold all the index cards
- A stereo and favorite CD

with the kinds of career choices they make. Mention the little tidbit about there being over 20,000 choices to pick from and use the following game to get them thinking about some of the options.

This game is a combination of Hot Potato and Charades. Give each student one or more index cards and ask them to write the name of a career on each card. Fold the cards in fourths and put them all into a large hat or box.

Have the students sit in a big circle—more than one circle if it's a large group—while you crank up the volume on a favorite CD. As long as the music plays, students pass the hat or box around the circle. When the music stops, the person with the hat or box picks a card, runs to the middle and acts out the profession. The music resumes when the group guesses the name of the profession. You can play for a few turns if time is short or until the hat or box is empty.

You'll need

- Extra copies of **So What Am I Gonna Do with My Life? Journaling Workbook for Students** for every student who doesn't have one yet

Allow time for small groups of students to get together and talk about the previous week's assignment in the journal. Small group time like this encourages participation and gives everyone time to talk through tough issues and interesting developments they encounter each week.

Give your students ample time to discuss their previous assignments in small groups, using questions like these:

- What's the most significant thing you read or thought or felt?
- Why do you suppose that seems important to you?
- What do you think you might want to do about that?

Direct your students to their journal assignment for the next week (pages 19-26 in the journal):

- **Holy Résumés** *Your students get a peek at the motley crew God hired to do his most important work.*
- **Mirror, Mirror on the Wall** *Your students can see who they really are—every reflection is fair!*
- **RIP** *Students step into the future for a moment and look back on the life they're about to live!*
- **Satisfaction Guaranteed** *God finishes what he starts—it's a promise!*
- **Dropping Hints** *The truth is out there. Students find out what their friends and family really think of them!*
- **Christians at Work** *Anna Quan—A Christian doctor who sees the instrument of true healing in God's love for people.*

You'll need

- Some time to research and organize Session 3 and your next **After Hours** event
- Resources to create the promotional material for these events, like a brief skit, video commercial, or flier
- The reproducible postcards provided on pages 69-75 (optional)

Promote the next session of **So What Am I Gonna Do with My Life?** and the upcoming **After Hours** event you have planned. See page 27 for details on the next session and pages 49-64 for **After Hours** ideas. Use a postcard from pages 65-75 to promote your activities.

Conclude the session by having students gather in groups of twos or threes to pray for each other as they continue their quests.

[One of a Kind]

I praise you because I am fearfully and wonderfully made; your works are wonderful, I know that full well. My frame was not hidden from you when I was made in the secret place. When I was woven together in the depths of the earth, your eyes saw my unformed body. All the days ordained for me were written in your book before one of them came to be.

—*Psalm 139:14-16*

Rewrite the verses using your owns words to clarify the idea that God has a hand in your destiny and a plan for your future.

[Vital Statistics]

Complete the following statements. When everyone in your group is finished, gather up the finished pages, put them in a pile, and take one at random that isn't your own. Take turns reading the answers out loud and guessing who wrote them.

My birthday is on—

I'm really good at—

I drive my parents crazy by—

The weirdest thing I ever did was—

When I was younger I wanted to be a—

MIND Your Mind, FOLLOW Your Heart, LISTEN to the Spirit

SESSION 3

The Big Plan

Listen to your heart and use your head to find God's will for your life.

The Whole Truth

- God loves you and always has your best interests at heart.
- Poor choices tend to leave you with fewer options and long-term complications.
- When signs such as wise counsel, personal desire, and circumstances come together, it's likely you're on the right track.

What the Good Book Says

- Psalm 37:3-5
- Proverbs 2:6-9
- Proverbs 3:3-6
- Proverbs 4:23-27
- Proverbs 16:3
- Proverbs 20:24
- Philippians 4:6-7
- James 4:13-17

Your Biblical Mentors

- David
- Elijah
- Lot
- Paul and Timothy

[The 411]

When figuring out what to do in life, do you follow your head or follow your heart? Generally, the best answer is *both*. Sometimes there's a big difference between what a person *wants* to do and what a person *thinks* he should do. One is driven by feelings, the other by facts. Both have an important role to play in making informed decisions about what to do in life. Unfortunately—in all too many cases—it's too much one way or the other. If a gal decides on a particular vocation because of the salary or because it's what her parents want—or some equally uninspired reason—the facts overpower dreams and desires. On the other hand, if a guy decides on a vocation he's completely unqualified for—one that's totally "against type"—that could indicate misplaced desires, and that's not good, either.

So as you guide your teens through this process, be aware that God not only uses the facts—abilities and talents—to lead them toward vocations, he uses those deep-down desires of the heart to guide their paths too—even if they seem wild or impossible.

Teach kids to take their dreams, run them through some time-honored tests, pray a lot, and then use the brains God gave them to do what they've got to do to make their dreams happen.

[Getting the Mood Right]

You might want to play music that will help your students process the key messages. Consider playing some of the following songs before, during, or after the session:

- "Give It Up" recorded by Avalon on the album *Avalon* (Sparrow, 1996)
- "My Will" recorded by DC Talk on the compilation album *Exodus* (Rocketown, 1998)
- "Trust" recorded by Sixpence None the Richer on the album *The Fatherless and the Widow* (R.E.X., 1993)

GOOFING OFF

HOW Do You Do and WHAT do you do?

Ask your students what are the two most common questions they use when meeting new people. The answers should be something like, *What's your name? Where do you live? What school do you attend?* Tell them as they become adults, getting acquainted with someone follows the same drill, except the questions change to something like, *What's your name? Where do you work? What do you do?*

> **You'll need**
> - Pencils
> - Copies of **How Do You Do and What Do You Do?** (page 34), one for each student
> - Adults to attend the first portion of your meeting

Give students copies of **How Do You Do and What Do You Do?** (page 34) and let them know they're going to get acquainted with some adults from the church using those two questions. (Depending on how civilized your group is, you may or may not want to role-play a socially acceptable way of introducing yourself to someone.)

Having prearranged details of the encounter with the pastor or an adult class leader, bring the two age groups together and let them mingle. (Have more adults than students for this activity, if possible.) The students should have the adults sign their names and write their job titles on the worksheet.

After about 10 minutes, pull your students together and thank the adults for coming. Take some time to talk about whom the teens met. They may be surprised to learn they've been going to church with all kinds of interesting people without realizing it.

WISHFUL thinking

With a bit of dramatic flair, announce that God has authorized you to act on his behalf and grant three wishes to each of the students in the room. The only restriction is the wishes have to concern the student's future and the student has to have a wholehearted desire for the wish.

Give your students copies of **Wishful Thinking** (page 35) and have them write down their three wishes. Have students share their wishes with two or three people around them.

Go for It!

*Using one of the following ideas might add some zing to **Wishful Thinking** —extra effort for added affect.*

- *Wear a turban and play the genie role for all it's worth.*
- *Show a video segment of the genie popping out of the bottle on "I Dream of Jeannie."*
- *Show the video segment approximately 30 minutes into Disney's Aladdin in which the genie explains his ability to grant wishes in the song "You Ain't Never Had a Friend Like Me."*

Dreaming of GENIE

Transition to this activity by mentioning that Christians sometimes treat God as if he were a wish-granting genie. It's not quite that simple, but one thing is certain: God has our best interests at heart. He wants us to have what we want as long as it's what *he* wants us to have.

[So what am I gonna do with my LIFE?]

To begin exploring this paradox, have three students read the following passages:

- Proverbs 3:5-6
- Psalm 37:4
- Matthew 7:7-8

After the students have read the passages, open discussion with questions like these:

- What promises does God make in these verses?
- What conditions does he state?
- How do you think these promises relate to you?
- How have you seen God fulfill these promises in your life or in the lives of people you know?

You can summarize the discussion by pointing out that God has made some pretty reassuring promises about taking care of our futures. Our job is to get to know him and learn to trust him more so *our* wishes are *his* wishes.

You want to get your students thinking about what happens when we don't trust him or follow his commands. What happens if we do things to mess up our lives? Throw out a couple specific scenarios to consider, but don't have them answer the questions yet.

- What about the teen who drives drunk and gets in a car wreck that leaves him paralyzed and kills his best friend?
- What about the couple who gets carried away and ends up with a baby they aren't ready to raise?
- What about the kid who…now ask your kids to name bad choices that could complicate their lives.

They'll probably name the biggies like drugs, murder, and stealing. But encourage them to consider more subtle problems like betraying confidences, deception (as opposed to outright lying), and gossip.

So what does happen if we goof up big time? This is one of the questions your students will consider next.

QUESTIONS of the HEART

You'll need

- Markers
- Three flipcharts and stands, large sheets of poster board, or 3 long sheets of butcher paper
- Tape
- Bibles
- One copy **Question of the Heart** (page 36), cut apart

Have three areas set up where students can make murals with markers on flipcharts, poster board, or butcher paper. Write one question from **Questions of the Heart** (page 36) at each location. Divide the group into three teams, sending one team to each area. They should discuss their assigned question briefly and then use the materials to turn their insights into artistic expression—anything from graffiti-like scribbling of Scripture references to stick-figure cartoons. Students can make their own individual contributions or work as a team on one colorful concept. Give them about 10 minutes to work on their mural, then rotate the groups to a new area. Give everyone a chance to discuss all three questions and add to all three murals.

Questions students will contemplate are—

- What happens if you do something to mess up your life?
- How do you know if an action is God's will?
- What can you do to make sure your thoughts and actions are in step with God's will?

NO TIME LIKE THE PRESENT

The BALL'S in your COURT

But there's another side to God's will. Maybe your students have heard people talk about "putting feet to their prayers." The saying means it's one thing to pray about a problem and another to do something about it. The same principle applies here.

God gave each of us a heart *and* a head. It's one thing to dream big dreams and want it with all your heart. It's quite another to do what you can to make it happen.

Read this story to your teens.

Delaney, a high school junior, wants to be a doctor. The idea was planted when she was a little girl playing hospital with her dolls. The interest grew as Delaney got older and worked as a candy

striper at the local hospital and volunteered at the first aid booth at the county fair. She's positive that becoming a doctor is what she wants to do with her life after watching doctors—with more than a little help from above—save the life of her older brother when he was in a car accident. Delaney has prayed about it, talked with people about it, used opportunities to check out the profession, and is convinced this is the best way to honor God with her life. No doubt about it, the dream and desire are all there.

Okay, Delaney knows what she wants to do with her life. Now all she has to do is wait for God to make things happen, right? *Wrong!* This is where her head takes over and she starts doing all she needs to do to make her dream come true. Like getting good grades—make that *exceptional* grades—in school and checking out colleges. But what else should someone in Delaney's shoes be doing?

After explaining Delaney's situation, turn the question to your students: What should *they* be doing to make their dreams come true? In **Wishful Thinking**, the students wrote down three things they really, really wanted in life—wanted with all their heart! Now there are a few questions they should be asking themselves. Share these with your students.

- Have you prayed about this idea, and do you have an unshakable peace in your heart that it's a good thing for your life?
- Have you talked about this idea with people whose opinions you value and had them encourage you to pursue it?
- Have you found or made opportunities that move you closer to realizing this goal or that allow you to learn more about it?
- Would a choice like this honor God?
- What can you do to move closer to realizing your goal?

You aren't necessarily asking these as questions for students to answer *now*. As you well know, a number of them have no idea what they want to do yet. This is a list of questions they should be asking—whenever God's will begins to come into focus for them. Summarize by sharing the bottom line with your students: *God gives the inspiration; we must give the perspiration.*

BUCKLING DOWN

Allow time for small groups of students to get together and talk about the previous week's assignments in *So What Am I Gonna Do with My Life? Journaling Workbook for Students*.

You'll need
- Extra copies—for those who don't have one yet—of *So What Am I Gonna Do with My Life? Journaling Workbook for Students*

Use questions like these—

- What's the most significant thing you read or thought or felt?
- Why do you suppose that seems important to you?
- What do you think you might want to do about that?

Small group time like this encourages participation and gives everyone time to talk through tough issues and interesting developments they encounter each week.

After giving your students ample time to discuss their previous assignments in small groups, give an overview of the upcoming journal assignments (pages 27-33 in the journal).

- **Fact or Fiction** *Dispelling some of the myths students might have about God's role in their futures.*
- **Heart Attack** *An opportunity for students to perform a self-check.*
- **Live and Learn** *The key to learning from mistakes.*
- **In God We Trust** *Learning to trust God with the future.*
- **Christians at Work** *Joe Markham—a guy who met his Maker and found his destiny making dog toys.*

You'll need

- Some time to research and organize the last session and your next **After Hours** event
- Resources to create the promotional material for these events, like a brief skit, video commercial, or flier
- The reproducible postcards provided on pages 65-75 (optional)

FUTURAMA

Promote the next session of *So What Am I Gonna Do with My Life?* and the upcoming **After Hours** event you have planned—perhaps through a brief skit, video commercial, or flier. See page 37 for details on the last session and pages 49-64 for **After Hours** ideas. Reproducible postcards for promotion are on pages 65-75.

THE FINISH LINE

Conclude this session by having students gather in groups of twos or threes to pray for each other as they continue their quests to find God's best for their lives.

How Do You Do and What Do You Do?

As you meet people during this event, be sure to keep track of their names and occupations on the chart below.

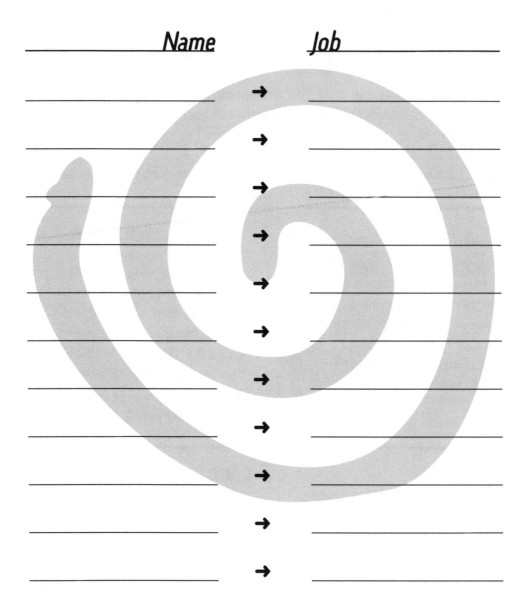

_____ *Name* _____ *Job* _____

→

→

→

→

→

→

→

→

→

→

→

Wishful Thinking

Here's your opportunity to put your dreams on paper. Imagine a genie standing in front of you, ready to give you anything you want for your future. There's just one catch—the genie will disappear back into the bottle after granting three wishes. So what are you gonna tell the genie?

The three wishes for my future are—

1.

2.

3.

[Questions of the Heart]

What happens if you do something to mess up your life?
Use Bible verses and examples to help you answer this question.

1

How can you tell if the desires of your heart are pleasing to God?
Use Bible verses and examples to help you answer this question.

2

Why do you think some Christians have the attitude that certain occupations
(for example, missionary or minister) are better than others?
Use Bible verses and examples to help you answer this question.

3

Getting your FEET WET

[The 411]

So far your students have focused mostly inward. Now it's time to take a turn. Time to find ways to put all they've learned to, umm, work. Time to seek some of those great opportunities lurking out there in the wonderful world of work.

The workplace—any workplace—offers a unique opportunity for Christians to let their lights shine. Students will have more credibility if they *live* the gospel by being the best, most dependable, most enjoyable, most motivated employees on the job. Encourage your teens to make good work ethics a part of their career goals. It will please their earthly bosses and honor their heavenly boss as well.

The Big Plan

Let your light shine in the workplace.

The Whole Truth

* *Seek out mentors and wise counsel within the church family.*
* *Give your best effort to every endeavor.*
* *Take every opportunity to do what's right.*
* *Learn practical skills to help reach your career goals.*

What the Good Book Says

* *Proverbs 15:22*
* *Proverbs 16:3*
* *Philippians 1:6*
* *Philippians 2:14-15*
* *Philippians 4:6-7, 19*
* *Colossians 3:23*
* *2 Thessalonians 3:6-13*

Your Biblical Mentors

* *Samuel and Eli*
* *Jesus and his disciples*
* *Paul and Barnabas*
* *Timothy, Eunice, and Lois*

[Getting the Mood Right]

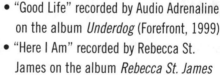

You might want to play music that will help your students process the key messages. Consider playing some of the following songs before, during, or after the session:

* "Hands and Feet" recorded by Audio Adrenaline on the album *Underdog* (Forefront, 1999)
* "Good Life" recorded by Audio Adrenaline on the album *Underdog* (Forefront, 1999)
* "Here I Am" recorded by Rebecca St. James on the album *Rebecca St. James* (Forefront, 1995)
* "Give It Up" recorded by Avalon on the album *Avalon* (Sparrow, 1996)

The Job HUNT

You'll need
- 15 church attenders, present at your class
- **Job Hunt** clues, gathered ahead of time
- Copies of **Job Hunt** (pages 43-44), one for each student
- Pencils

To prepare for this lesson, invite 15 adults from your church (representing a variety of occupations) to be present. Find out interesting facts about each occupation and write a brief riddle-style clue. A clue for a doctor might be, "Take two aspirin and call me in the morning." For a sanitation engineer you might write, "One man's trash is another man's treasure." Record them on **Job Hunt** (pages 43-44) and make copies for the meeting.

Ask your guests to arrive a little early, so they're all present when students begin trickling in. When your teens arrive, hand them a copy of **Job Hunt** (with only the clues listed; names and occupations are left blank). Let them mingle with the guests and ask questions about their work until they figure out who's who and what they do.

When most students are finished, take a few minutes to briefly introduce your guests and identify their professions. If you have enough time, ask them to share their best advice about finding the right vocation—in 25 words or less.

KICKING THINGS OFF

Back TRACK

You'll need
- Pencils
- Index cards

Try a twist on charades to review the messages from the past few weeks.
Divide the group into two (or more) teams and send them to separate areas of the room. Give each team about 15 index cards and ask them to write phrases, verses (paraphrased in their own words is fine), and biblical stories that they've learned over the past several weeks—one idea per card. Have each team gather its cards, shuffle 'em a bit, and turn them over to the other team, face down. The two teams will be playing at the same time, but separately.

After you give the signal, the first person on each team acts out the top card in the stack, and the team member who guesses correctly then grabs the next card and acts it out. The teams race against each other to see which team can guess the most cards before you let them know time is up.

Road RULES

You'll need

- Copies of **Road Rules** (page 45)—one for each student (or make a transparency or PowerPoint slide or copy it onto butcher paper for all to see)

Work. Life-sustaining, unavoidable, sometimes enjoyable, pain-in-the-neck *work*.

It's where your students will spend a big chunk of their adult lives and where they'll be challenged to live out their faith. Work environments are often competitive, stressful, even hostile—hardly ideal circumstances for exuding the fruit of the Spirit, and yet the very places we need to let our light shine.

Using **Road Rules** (page 45), review three important rules they should be aware of:

- Don't try to do it alone.
- Give everything your best shot.
- Dare to do the impossible.

Let your students interact with these ideas during the next activity.

Office SUPPLIES

You'll need

- Markers
- Three large sheets of poster board
- A colorful assortment of construction paper
- Craft supplies
- Scissors
- Tape
- One copy of **Office Supplies** (page 46), cut apart

Before the session begins gather three large sheets of poster board along with some other craft supplies: markers, construction paper, yarn, scissors, tape. Divide the class into three groups and distribute the supplies. Give each group one of the rules from **Office Supplies** (page 46).

Each group should use its rule and the accompanying verse to design stationery, a work uniform, or a work-related accessory to apply the principle to a real-life work situation. Have the students use the craft supplies to make a mock-up of their idea on the poster board, complete with a title and instructions for use.

If your teens need an example to get their creative juices flowing, you might mention how doing your best work could be illustrated with an imaginary product called a Best-O-Meter—a watch that sets off an alarm when it senses that you are not doing your best at work.

When the groups have the models complete, stage a mock business meeting where representatives from the various groups can pitch their product to the other teams, explaining its significance and relevance to the rule and verse.

NO TIME LIKE THE PRESENT

Presenting ME!

You'll need
- Copies of **Presenting Me!** (page 47)—one for each student (or make it into a transparency or PowerPoint slide or copy it onto butcher paper)

We've talked about what the Big Boss says about work and success. But what about the other bosses, like your future employers? What do they want you to bring to the job besides great skills? Employers look for three things in particular.

- Employees who have good interpersonal skills, like the abilities to be courteous and to communicate clearly
- Employees who are dependable
- Employees who take initiative

Ethical Employees

For more information about ethics in the workplace, including two self-scoring work ethic inventories, go to www.coe.uga.edu/workethic.

Take a few minutes to guide the group in a discussion about what these three traits mean, especially in light of their Christian faith. How do these traits relate to what the Bible tells us should already be part of a Christian's character?

Give your students an opportunity to practice all three skills. This quick and almost painless exercise gives your students a chance to work in a group, gives them an opportunity to practice effective communication, gives them chances to encourage others, and forces them out of their comfort zones. It's a mini-exercise in building interpersonal skills, showing some dependability, and taking initiative! Have the group break into teams of three to five people. Each person completes the statements on **Presenting Me!** (page 47) in an impromptu and informal presentation for the rest of the small group.

- As a career, I think God wants me to...
- To get ready, I am...
- In this career I hope to accomplish...

BUCKLING DOWN

You'll need
- Extra copies—for those who don't have one yet—of *So What Am I Gonna Do with My Life? Journaling Workbook for Students*

Allow time for small groups of students to talk about the previous week's journal assignment. Small group time like this encourages participation and gives everyone time to talk through tough issues and interesting developments.

After giving your students ample time to discuss their previous assignments in small groups, tell them what they'll be doing this week in their journals (pages 34-42 in the journal). You'll need to plan a time to let your students debrief about the assignment.

- **Way to Go** *A closer look at the options and a chance to take a crack at making plans for the future.*
- **Two Heads Are Better Than One** *Getting an edge on success by adding these ingredients to the planning process.*
- **If You Were Me** *Finding out what others might do if they were in the students' shoes.*
- **Why Not You?** *Destined for greatness or destined to do a great job at whatever they chose to do? Your students will find out here.*
- **The Good Life** *Finding out what else God wants in your students' futures.*
- **Christians at Work** *Tom Mahairas—an ex-hippie/ex-druggie who took God at his word and got more adventure than he bargained for.*

FUTURAMA

Promote any additional activities you might have planned. See pages 49-64 for **After Hours** ideas. Reproducible promotional postcards are on pages 65-75.

[*You'll need*
- Time to research and organize your upcoming **After Hours** event
- The resources to create the promotional material for these events, like a brief skit, video commercial, or flier
- The reproducible postcards provided on pages 65-75 (optional)]

THE FINISH LINE

Conclude this session by having students gather in groups of twos or threes to pray for each other as they continue their quests.

[The Job Hunt]

Be a detective. Each clue represents one of our mystery guests and his or her occupation. Ask questions of these mysterious members of the work force to find out who they are and what they do.

Clue	Name	Profession
His company car is big, yellow, and stops at train tracks	Gabriel Ortiz	Bus driver
1.		
2.		
3.		
4.		
5.		
6.		
7.		

(continued)

[The Job Hunt]

Be a detective. Each clue represents one of our mystery guests and his or her occupation. Ask questions of these mysterious members of the work force to find out who they are and what they do.

Clue	Name	Profession
8.		
9.		
10.		
11.		
12.		
13.		
14.		
15.		

(page 2)

Don't try to do it alone.

Give everything your best shot.

Dare to do the impossible.

[Office Supplies]

Don't try to do it alone.

Plans fail for lack of counsel, but with many advisors they succeed. —*Proverbs 15:22*

Use the materials provided to create stationery, a work uniform, or a work-related accessory to illustrate how this principle and verse can be put into action in the workplace.

- -

Give everything your best shot.

Whatever you do, work at it with all your heart, as working for the Lord, not for men. —*Colossians 3:23*

Use the materials provided to create stationery, a work uniform, or a work-related accessory to illustrate how this principle and verse can be put into action in the workplace.

- -

Dare to do the impossible.

I can do everything through him who gives me strength. —*Philippians 4:13*

Use the materials provided to create stationery, a work uniform, or a work-related accessory to illustrate how this principle and verse can be put into action in the workplace.

[Presenting Me!]

- For a career, I think God wants me to…

- To get ready, I am…

- In this career I hope to accomplish…

Save room for the SMORGASBORD!

If your teens are using **So What Am I Gonna Do with My Life? Journaling Workbook for Students**, you can direct them to pages 43-50 for additional activities and for pages that may be used instead of the handouts in the Leader's Guide.

TOP 25

You'll need
- Whiteboard
- Markers

It's pretty common among people—young and old alike—to know of about 25 different career options. But the fact is there are over 20,000 options to choose from. Thus, the first task of this **After Hours** session is to get your students

20,000 and Counting

Curious about those 20,000 career options? Go to the library and pick up a copy of the U.S. Department of Labor's Dictionary of Occupational Titles, where you'll find descriptions of everything from apiculturist to zoologist. The most recent edition is usually kept in the reference section, but ask the librarian for older editions that might be available for checkout.

to think beyond the obvious vocations of doctor, lawyer, teacher, and scientist. And your more spiritually minded students should start looking further than pastor, missionary, or youth leader.

To get the activity rolling, have the group brainstorm a list of careers for Christians, which you can jot down for everyone to see. Have students call out the first ideas that pop into their heads.

Keep the process snappy by not letting teens criticize the ideas of others. Stop when you get to 25 ideas. This list becomes the group's "common list."

If the list seems top-heavy with straight-from-Sunday-school responses, take a few minutes to discuss the legitimacy of honoring God through any work choice that doesn't compromise a Christian's values, beliefs, and legal obligations.

O N   A   R O L L

Now the goal is to edge your list a bit closer to the 20,000 mark. Divide the group into teams of five to 10 players. Give each team a marker and a roll of toilet paper—the stiffer and scratchier, the better. Tell them to think of as many different career ideas as they can—excluding the 25 already mentioned—and write one idea per square on their roll.(Keep them connected.) Give them about 10 minutes to brainstorm and then call everyone back together.

Let each team unfurl its roll and read the list out loud. The team with the longest list wins. Award the winning team a toilet brush or some other tacky memento of the activity.

> ### You'll need
> - A roll of toilet paper for each team
> - A washable marker for each team
> - A prize for the winning team

G E T   T H E E   T O   A   L I B R A R Y !

Have the kids choose one toilet paper square each that lists a career they'd like to consider for themselves. (Or they can write new ones if they'd prefer).

Remind them that the best decisions are informed decisions, so you're giving them a chance to find out details about various careers via the good old-fashioned library.

It's your call whether you want to take the students to the library or bring the library to them. If your local public or school library can accommodate a group of students without going crazy, make arrangements with the librarian to invade. If not—or if you prefer a more relaxed approach—gather up as many books on careers as you can and bring them to your kids. **Check It Out!** (page 54) has suggestions of where to find helpful material and the titles of specific books you may want to look for.

Pass out copies of **Get Thee to a Library!** (pages 52-53) and give the students half an hour or so to find the designated information. If you're in your own space, add munchies and some background music and let them go to it.

> ### You'll need
> - Pencils
> - The rolls of toilet paper used in the previous activity
> - A variety of career books or transportation to the library)
> - Copies of **Get Thee to a Library!** and **Check It Out!** (pages 52-54), one for each student
> - Munchies (optional)
> - A stereo and a favorite CD (optional)

You'll need

[
- The students' completed worksheets from the previous activity
]

Bring the group back together and remind them just because a career sounds great on paper, doesn't mean it's great for every individual. Break students up into groups of five to 10 and let them share the information they found. Give each student a chance to briefly describe to the rest of the group what was discovered about this career choice.

Let others in the group ask questions and take a jury-style vote on whether or not the career seems like a good fit for the student. Ask the groups to compare the jury's vote with the student's own conclusion and discuss any differences. Are the students still interested in the careers they researched? Did the information they gathered change how they feel about those careers?

You'll need

[
- Copies of **Surf's Up!** (pages 55-56), one for each student
]

These kids have been blessed with the greatest source of information since Moses came down from the mountain with stone tablets—the Internet. It's the number one spot for career resources, college searches, and job hunts. There's no better place to find fascinating facts about all kinds of professions.

The Internet is a great place for students to continue their searches for career information. Give them a copy of **Surf's Up!** (pages 55-56) and encourage them to continue their search for just the right job online.

In case you just can't let 'em loose without a devotion, take a few minutes to share Paul's prayer for the Colossians.

> **For this reason, since the day we heard about you, we have not stopped praying for you and asking God to fill you with the knowledge of his will through all spiritual wisdom and understanding. And we pray this in order that you might live a life worthy of the Lord and may please him in every way: bearing fruit in every good work, growing in the knowledge of God.**
> **—*Colossians 1:9-10***

Make this your prayer for each of your students and ask them to pair up to personalize the prayer for each other... "Fill Ian with the knowledge of your will..."

[Get Thee to a Library!]

Pick a career you want to know more about and write it here—

*Now explore the library or the resources available to find out more about your chosen profession. The resources listed on **Check It Out!** will help you.*

So what about that career you've researched...

1. What do people working in this profession do all day?

2. What kinds of skills do they use on the job?

3. What education and training do they need?

4. What kinds of employers hire people to do this kind of work? List names of companies if you find them.

5. How much money does a person make in this profession when starting out?

(continued)

Get Thee to a Library!

6. What opportunities are available for people in this profession as they gain more experience and training?

7. How much demand is expected for this type of worker in the next 10 years?

8. What careers are similar to this one but require less training? That require more training?

9. What abilities and interests do you have that might make this career a good fit for you?

10. How would a job like this allow you to honor God with your work?

Is this career for you?

❏ Yes! This is it! I'm going to trust God to open doors and seee where it takes me.

❏ No! Anything but this!

❏ Maybe. This one sounds interesting, but I need more information before I decide.

(page 2)

[Check It Out!]

- Check out the books with call numbers *331.702*—this is where you'll find general career information about all kinds of careers. A great place to start the search.
- Explore the reference section with call numbers *331.702*—sometimes the best stuff is in this section. You can't check out these books, so bring some change to pay for copies of information you want to keep.
- Look up topics such as *engineering* or *healthcare* when you want to get more in-depth information about a specific profession.

And You Won't Want to Miss...

The Adams Job Almanac edited by Adam Graber (Adams Media Corp., 1999)
America's Top 300 Jobs edited by J. Michael Farr (Jist Books, 2000)
Cool Careers for Dummies by Marty Nemko with Paul and Sarah Edwards (1998)

100 Best Careers for the 21st Century by Shelly Field (2000)
100 Jobs in the Environment by Debra Quintana (1997)
100 Jobs in Social Change by Harley Jebens (1997)
100 Jobs in Technology by Lori Hawkins and Betsy Dowling (1997)
100 Jobs in Words by Scott A. Meyer (1997)
—all published by IDG Books Worldwide

The following books contain excellent information on careers, although they're written for slightly younger readers

Career Ideas for Kids Who Like Animals & Nature (2000)
Career Ideas for Kids Who Like Art (1998)
Career Ideas for Kids Who Like Computers (1998)
Career Ideas for Kids Who Like Math (2000)
Career Ideas for Kids Who Like Science (1998)
Career Ideas for Kids Who Like Sports (1998)
Career Ideas for Kids Who Like Talking (1998)
Career Ideas for Kids Who Like Writing (1998)
—all by Diane Lindsey Reeves (Checkmark Books)

Cool Careers for Girls in Air & Space (2000)
Cool Careers for Girls in Computers (1999)
Cool Careers for Girls in Construction (2000)
Cool Careers for Girls in Engineering (1999)
Cool Careers for Girls in Food (1999)
Cool Careers for Girls in Health (1999)
Cool Careers for Girls in Law (2000)
Cool Careers for Girls in Performing Arts (2000)
Cool Careers for Girls in Sports (1999)
Cool Careers for Girls with Animals (1999)
—all by Ceel Pasternak and Linda Thornburg (Impact Publishing)

[Surf's Up!]

Lucky you! You're the first generation to have access to the wonders of the Internet. Anything you could possibly want to know—about nearly anything—you can find with a few clicks. Try it. Career information, college applications, job-hunting—it's all there!

So pick a career—any career that might interest you—and see whether you can find the following information. Write down the exact Web site address for each site you visit and print out pages with information you want to keep.

Profession

Profile of the profession

College or training program to get prepared for this career

(continued)

[Surf's Up!]

Professional associations

Employers who hire people in this profession

Hot trends or current projects in this profession

Here are some sites you may want to visit:

careerideasforkids.com   careermag.com

careermosaic.com   careerpathsonline.com

careerplanning.about.com   futurescan.com

ivillage.com/career   review.com

(page 2)

Grabbing TRIED and TRUE tips from FAMILIAR faces

If your teens are using *So What Am I Gonna Do with My Life? Journaling Workbook for Students*, you can direct them to pages 51-52 for additional activities.

THE IDEA

Yes, it's a career fair—but with a twist! Instead of strangers, the people sharing their work experiences will be members of the church. These are people who care about the ultimate success of your youth. People who are willing to surround these teens with support, advice, and prayers.

To visualize this churchwide fair, start with an idea of the typical high school career day—yawn—and add several ingredients that will combine to make it effective, enjoyable, and a means to enhance intergenerational relationships within the church family. The event consists of several individual, small group, and large group activities.

SHOE SWAP

You'll need
- Pencils
- One adult for every teen
- Copies of **Shoe Swap** (page 60), cut up, one card for each person

Give each person—young and old alike—a **Shoe Swap** (page 60) game card that says "If I were in your shoes…"

Ask everyone to write some advice to the opposite generation—teens write to adults, adults write to teens—about making the most out of life.

Have the teens remove one shoe each and place them in a pile, where the adults will fill the shoes with their cards. Have adults remove one shoe each and place them in another pile, where the teens will fill the shoes with their cards. (Try to work with an even number of adults and teens, so no one gets left out.) Now jumble all the shoes together—teens' and adults'—and give the old "Ready, set, go!" Let everyone scramble to find their shoe and read the tidbit of advice inside from the other generation.

HELP WANTED

Set up a bulletin board area to post information and appointment signups, if you're using appointments. Give adults who are offering jobs, apprenticeships, or mentoring opportunities places at the tables for one-on-one discussions with teens. You may want to make signs that identify the business or type of opportunity to place nearby. Kids can sign up or wait for openings. You may also want to gather up job applications from local businesses and have tables available where students can fill out the forms and

You'll need
- Bulletin boards and push pins
- Paper, pens, and pencils
- Tables and chairs
- Adults offering jobs, apprenticeships, or mentoring opportunities
- Signs as needed
- Extra adult volunteers
- Job applications from local businesses

get advice from adult volunteers if needed. Give your students free time to cruise this area as well as the **Show and Tell** booths (described next).

SHOW AND TELL

Set up booths or tables where church members—and community employers, if desired—can showcase their occupations. Encourage exhibitors to make their booths as visually appealing as possible by displaying posters describing their occupa-

You'll need
- Booths or tables for exhibits
- Adults willing to showcase their occupations

tions and how they make a difference in the world (all occupations make a difference when you think about it). They can make their displays interactive by bringing products, showing the work they do and the tools they use, and offering hands-on projects for students to try.

You'll need

- Adults willing to be interviewed about their occupations
- Chairs

Arrange for three to five people with interesting jobs—from the church or community—to be available for group interviews. Assign your volunteers to their own separate areas with chairs set up for students.

Call your students together and divide them into as many groups as there are interviewees. Students are free to ask any career-related questions, but you may want to offer suggestions like these:

- How did you chose your career?
- What did you do to prepare for your career?
- What do you like about your career?
- What do you dislike about your career?

If you have more than three or four interviewees, you might want to color-code the locations and provide students with color-coded tickets—strips of colored construction paper will do. Rotate the location colors and have students go to the new location of their assigned color.

Designate one teen from each group to ask the first question and challenge the other students to keep the questions rolling.

Call time after about 10 minutes and have the groups rotate to new areas. Repeat this process as often as time allows or until the groups have rotated through every interview area.

You'll need

- Munchies
- A stereo and some favorite CDs

Bring on the food and crank up the music. Wrap up the session with time for networking. Encourage teens to talk further to adults with careers they're interested in.

[Shoe Swap]

If I were in your
YOUR SHOES...

If I were in your
YOUR SHOES...

If I were in your
YOUR SHOES...

If I were in your
YOUR SHOES...

If I were in your
YOUR SHOES...

If I were in your
YOUR SHOES...

Only the SHADOW knows...

Field trips to workplaces where students actually experience a realistic day on the job is called *job shadowing*. Depending on your resources you can go several ways with a job-shadowing event.

> *If your teens are using So What Am I Gonna Do with My Life? Journaling Workbook for Students, you can direct them to pages 53-54 for additional activities.*

- Arrange—or have students arrange—to visit a workplace of their choice, on their own or in pairs.
- Arrange for a group field trip to a major employer in the area (hospital, television station, sports stadium, factory).
- Arrange for students to accompany adults of the church to work.

Adding a hands-on work experience can be a real plus. It's a win-win situation. The adult worker helps the students by sharing their time and expertise, and the student may be able to help the adult worker by lending a hand in a project.

ALL IN A DAY'S WORK

You'll need
- Prearranged workplaces for every student to visit
- Cards from **All in a Day's Work** (page 63), filled out for each student
- A place to meet and debrief after the workplace visits
- Maps (optional)
- Transportation (optional)

At your youth group meeting immediately prior to the date for this event, pass out assignment cards from **All in a Day's Work** (page 63) and make sure students know where they're going as well as when and where they're supposed to link up with the rest of the group.

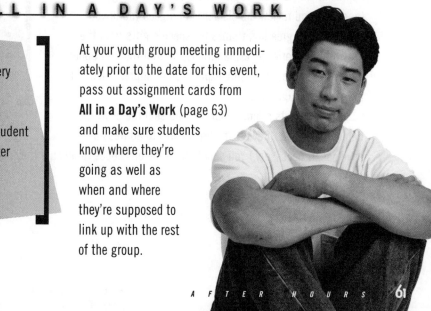

Visits of two to three hours are usually ample for the first time out.

Before you leave set up a contest to bring back the most unusual souvenir from the workplace. All souvenirs should be approved by their work-place hosts!

Go through the mind-your-manners drill, and tell your students all you can about what to expect from the experience. Arrange to meet at your specified location at the specified time for debriefing.

If you take all your students to the same location, the assignment cards aren't needed, but prearranged transportation to and from the workplace will be.

YOU MEAN YOU GET PAID FOR THIS?

After everyone gets back to the rendezvous point, provide some munchies and a chance to chat about their experiences. Be sure to let teens show their souvenirs and award the prize for most unusual.

You'll need
- Munchies

WE'RE MUCH OBLIGED!

Make sure to follow-up with this important gesture of appreciation. Pass out copies of **We're Much Obliged!** (page 64) and review the elements of a good thank-you note: a proper greeting, thanks for specific gifts from the host (time, experience, explanations), a brief thought about a benefit received, a closing expression of appreciation, and the student's signature.

Have students stamp, address, and seal the envelopes before they leave. (Review the proper way to address an envelope, if necessary.) You should mail the envelopes to be sure they actually get sent.

You'll need
- Pens
- Thank-you notes
- Copies of **We're Much Obliged!** (page 64), one for each student
- Stamps

[All in a Day's Work]

Contact name_____

Business name _____

Business phone number _____

Directions to workplace _____

Your visit is scheduled from _____ to _____

Meet us back at _____ by _____

- ✂ -

Contact name_____

Business name _____

Business phone number _____

Directions to workplace _____

Your visit is scheduled from _____ to _____

Meet us back at _____ by _____

- -

Contact name_____

Business name _____

Business phone number _____

Directions to workplace _____

Your visit is scheduled from _____ to _____

Meet us back at _____ by _____

- -

Contact name_____

Business name _____

Business phone number _____

Directions to workplace _____

Your visit is scheduled from _____ to _____

Meet us back at _____ by _____

Thank you!

April 23, 2006

Dear Mr. Washburn,

Thank you for letting me join you at work today. I never realized newspaper work is so demanding. My experience with you helped me realize I might like to be a reporter someday. Thanks for sharing your time and knowledge with me.

Sincerely,

Valena Wilcox

The BUZZ factor

GETTIN' THE WORD OUT

Whether your youth group is large or small, good communication is key. The postcards on pages 66-73 can be used to advertise any of these activities. Just fill in the vital stats and copy away! Could it be any easier?

Of course the **After Hours** activities will require more than a little cooperation from the adult population of your church. Don't assume these important volunteers will come to you—go to them! Put something in their hands! Put something in their mailboxes! *Promote, promote, promote* until you get the help you need to make your **After Hours** activities a success. Use the postcards and fliers on pages 66-75 to stir up adult participation.

So warm up the copier, load it with colored paper or cardstock, and pray your machine can survive the workout!

[Postcards]

✂

Where?

When?

What?

---

fold ——————————————————————————————————— *fold*

So What are You Gonna Do With Your Life?

Get the inside scoop.
God knows. Do you?

where...

when...

what...

fold

fold

Hey Kid!

Get a Life!
Find out how...

[Postcards]

where...

when...

what...

Hey hey, kid...

Has God got a plan for you!

Find out what it is!

Where...

when...

What...

fold   *fold*

Whatcha
wanna be
when you
grow up?
Let God help you
figure it out.
Find out how.

[Postcards]

where...

when...

what...

WHaTCHa waNNa Be

WHEN YOU

grow up?

LET GOD HELP YOU FIGURE IT OUT. **fiND OUT HOW.**

fold

fold

[Postcards]

Let kids learn from your success.
Let them learn from your mistakes.

To find out how you can get involved, contact

Where

When

fold

fold

When I Grow Up.

You made that decision years ago. Or did you?
What have you learned along the way?
Our young people need to know.
Share your experiences at

**Grabbing Tried and True Tips
from Familiar Faces**

[Postcards]

Your story can make a difference.

To find out more, contact

Where

When

fold ⋮ fold

Everybody has a story.
Yours could change young lives.

What's your story? The one about how you make a living. Is God using you in some weird and wonderful ways on the job? Have you learned some valuable lessons from the school of hard knocks? Do you know a thing or two about what it takes to let your light shine in the workplace?

   Don't keep it to yourself! Pass on your experience to the next generation.

Join us for
Grabbing Tried and True Tips from familiar faces

[Postcards]

Let them learn from your mistakes.

Let kids learn from your success.

To find out how you can
get involved, contact

Where

When

fold

fold

When
I Grow Up.

You made that decision years ago. Or did you?
What have you learned along the way?
Our young people need to know.
Share your experiences at

Grabbing Tried and True Tips from Familiar Faces

[Help Wanted!]

Wanted: Church family and friends willing to invest in the lives of teens. Willingness to share your experiences in the workplace a must. Blue-collar, white-collar, pink-collar—all are welcome and encouraged to apply! Heavenly dividends guaranteed!

Positions Available

❏ I'd love to set up a display showcasing what I do on the job.

❏ I'd love to let teens pick my brain about my job in a group interview.

❏ I'd be glad to let a teen tag along with me on the job for a couple of hours.

❏ I'd love to put a teen to work with a part-time job, internship, or temporary assignment.

❏ I'd love to help set up the celebration.

❏ I'd love to come. Let me know other ways I can help.

❏ I can't come, but I can help with behind-the-scenes work.

❏ I'd love to drive. Let me know if anyone needs a ride.

❏ I'd love to help with food.

Name _____

Phone _____

E-mail _____

If you're interested in showcasing your occupation, please fill out the information below.

Employer _____

Occupation _____

Comments _____

_____

_____

[Help Wanted!]

Wanted: Church family and friends willing to invest in the lives of teens. Willingness to share your experiences in the workplace a must. Blue-collar, white-collar, pink-collar-all are welcome and encouraged to apply! Heavenly dividends guaranteed!

Positions Available

○ I'd love to set up a display showcasing what I do on the job.

○ I'd love to let teens pick my brain about my job in a group interview.

○ I'd be glad to let a teen tag along with me on the job for a couple of hours.

○ I'd love to put a teen to work with a part-time job, internship, or temporary assignment.

○ I'd love to help set up the celebration.

○ I'd love to come. Let me know other ways I can help.

○ I can't come, but I can help with behind-the-scenes work.

○ I'd love to drive. Let me know if anyone needs a ride.

○ I'd love to help with food.

Name _____

Phone _____

E-mail _____

If you're interested in showcasing your occupation, please fill out the information below.

Employer _____

Occupation _____

Comments _____
_____
_____

Resources from YOUTH SPECIALTIES

Youth Ministry Programming

Camps, Retreats, Missions, & Service Ideas (Ideas Library)

Compassionate Kids: Practical Ways to Involve Your Students in Mission and Service

Creative Bible Lessons from the Old Testament

Creative Bible Lessons in 1 & 2 Corinthians

Creative Bible Lessons in John: Encounters with Jesus

Creative Bible Lessons in Romans: Faith on Fire!

Creative Bible Lessons on the Life of Christ

Creative Bible Lessons in Psalms

Creative Junior High Programs from A to Z, Vol. 1 (A-M)

Creative Junior High Programs from A to Z, Vol. 2 (N-Z)

Creative Meetings, Bible Lessons, & Worship Ideas (Ideas Library)

Crowd Breakers & Mixers (Ideas Library)

Downloading the Bible Leader's Guide

Drama, Skits, & Sketches (Ideas Library)

Drama, Skits, & Sketches 2 (Ideas Library)

Dramatic Pauses

Everyday Object Lessons

Games (Ideas Library)

Games 2 (Ideas Library)

Good Sex: A Whole-Person Approach to Teenage Sexuality & God

Great Fundraising Ideas for Youth Groups

More Great Fundraising Ideas for Youth Groups

Great Retreats for Youth Groups

Holiday Ideas (Ideas Library)

Hot Illustrations for Youth Talks

More Hot Illustrations for Youth Talks

Still More Hot Illustrations for Youth Talks

Ideas Library on CD-ROM

Incredible Questionnaires for Youth Ministry

Junior High Game Nights

More Junior High Game Nights

Kickstarters: 101 Ingenious Intros to Just about Any Bible Lesson

Live the Life! Student Evangelism Training Kit

Memory Makers

The Next Level Leader's Guide

Play It! Over 150 Great Games for Youth Groups

Roaring Lambs

So What Am I Gonna Do with My Life? Leader's Guide

Special Events (Ideas Library)

Spontaneous Melodramas

Spontaneous Melodramas 2

Student Leadership Training Manual

Student Underground: An Event Curriculum on the Persecuted Church

Super Sketches for Youth Ministry

Talking the Walk

Videos That Teach

What Would Jesus Do? Youth Leader's Kit

Wild Truth Bible Lessons

Wild Truth Bible Lessons 2

Wild Truth Bible Lessons—Pictures of God

Wild Truth Bible Lessons—Pictures of God 2

Worship Services for Youth Groups

Professional Resources

Administration, Publicity, & Fundraising (Ideas Library)

Dynamic Communicators Workshop for Youth Workers

Equipped to Serve: Volunteer Youth Worker Training Course

Help! I'm a Junior High Youth Worker!

Help! I'm a Small-Group Leader!

Help! I'm a Sunday School Teacher!

Help! I'm a Volunteer Youth Worker!

How to Expand Your Youth Ministry

How to Speak to Youth...and Keep Them Awake at the Same Time

Junior High Ministry (Updated & Expanded)

The Ministry of Nurture: A Youth Worker's Guide to Discipling Teenagers

Postmodern Youth Ministry

Purpose-Driven Youth Ministry

Purpose-Driven Youth Ministry Training Kit

So *That's* Why I Keep Doing This! 52 Devotional Stories for Youth Workers

Teaching the Bible Creatively

A Youth Ministry Crash Course

Youth Ministry Management Tools

The Youth Worker's Handbook to Family Ministry

Academic Resources

Four Views of Youth Ministry and the Church

Starting Right: Thinking Theologically about Youth Ministry

Discussion Starters

Discussion & Lesson Starters (Ideas Library)

Discussion & Lesson Starters 2 (Ideas Library)

EdgeTV

Get 'Em Talking

Keep 'Em Talking!

Good Sex: A Whole-Person Approach to Teenage Sexuality & God

High School TalkSheets

More High School TalkSheets

High School TalkSheets from Psalms and Proverbs

Junior High TalkSheets

More Junior High TalkSheets

Junior High TalkSheets from Psalms and Proverbs

Real Kids: Short Cuts

Real Kids: The Real Deal—on Friendship, Loneliness, Racism, & Suicide

Real Kids: The Real Deal—on Sexual Choices, Family Matters, & Loss

Real Kids: The Real Deal—on Stressing Out, Addictive Behavior, Great Comebacks, & Violence

Real Kids: Word on the Street

Unfinished Sentences: 450 Tantalizing Statement-Starters to Get Teenagers Talking & Thinking

What If...? 450 Thought-Provoking Questions to Get Teenagers Talking, Laughing, and Thinking

Would You Rather...? 465 Provocative Questions to Get Teenagers Talking

Have You Ever...? 450 Intriguing Questions Guaranteed to Get Teenagers Talking

Art Source Clip Art

Stark Raving Clip Art (print)

Youth Group Activities (print)

Clip Art Library Version 2.0 (CD-ROM)

Digital Resources

Clip Art Library Version 2.0 (CD-ROM)

Ideas Library on CD-ROM

Youth Ministry Management Tools (CD-ROM)

Videos & Video Curricula

Dynamic Communicators Workshop for Youth Workers

EdgeTV

Equipped to Serve: Volunteer Youth Worker Training Course

Good Sex: A Whole-Person Approach to Teenage Sexuality & God

The Heart of Youth Ministry: A Morning with Mike Yaconelli

Live the Life! Student Evangelism Training Kit

Purpose-Driven Youth Ministry Training Kit

Real Kids: Short Cuts

Real Kids: The Real Deal—on Friendship, Loneliness, Racism, & Suicide

Real Kids: The Real Deal—on Sexual Choices, Family Matters, & Loss

Real Kids: The Real Deal—on Stressing Out, Addictive Behavior, Great Comebacks, & Violence

Real Kids: Word on the Street

Student Underground: An Event Curriculum on the Persecuted Church

Understanding Your Teenager Video Curriculum

Student Resources

Downloading the Bible: A Rough Guide to the New Testament

Downloading the Bible: A Rough Guide to the Old Testament

Grow For It Journal

Grow For It Journal through the Scriptures

So What Am I Gonna Do with My Life? Journaling Workbook for Students

Spiritual Challenge Journal: The Next Level

Teen Devotional Bible

What Almost Nobody Will Tell You about Sex

What Would Jesus Do? Spiritual Challenge Journal

Wild Truth Journal for Junior Highers

Wild Truth Journal—Pictures of God